*Synonym
for Home*

Poems

Michelle Murphy

Wet Cement Press
Berkeley, California

Copyright© 2019 Michelle Murphy
All rights reserved

ISBN: 978-1-7324369-2-3

Wet Cement Press
Berkeley, California

www.wetcementpress.com
wetcementpress@gmail.com

Cover drawing by Sheridan Jones,
a self-portrait artist and photographer living
in the Cotswolds in the United Kingdom.

Acknowledgments:
Thank you to the editors of the following publications in which some of these poems first appeared: *Barzakh!, Zen Monster #3, The American Journal of Poetry, (b)OINK, Marsh Hawk Review* and *Galatea Resurrects*. Special thanks to VERSE Volume 33, in which a portfolio of these poems was selected as a finalist for the 2015 Tomaž Šalamun Prize.

WCP3-2

Contents

Part 1
Confabulation	1
Synonym for Home	2
Ways	5
What Lies Beneath	6
Compass	7

Part 2
Vanishing Twin	11
Vagrant Waltz	12
Rift	13
Relativity Once Removed	15
Tale	17
Daughters	18
For Ann	19
Topology	20

Part 3
Instructions for the Eclipse	25
Impediment	26
Steer Clear	27
Dinghy	28
Tumble Down	30
Keep Rising	31
Flood Zone	32
Rough Draft for April	33
Intermezzo & Single Tanka	34

Hem	37
Open Space	38
Keep It Together	39
Empty Your Pockets	40
Underscore	42
Little Bombs	43
There/Enough	44
Heresy	48
Year of the Bumblebee	49
Four-Minute Warning	50
Wyrd	51
Recitation	53
Church	56

Part 4

How to Canter Under Anesthesia	61
Radiotherapy	63
27th Letter	65
Perch	67
Anywhere At All	68
An Undoing	69
She Took Off Her Girdle	71

About the Author	75
Wet Cement Press Titles	77

Thank you, as always, to my remarkable husband and soul mate, Eric, and to our daughters, Grace and Hayley who have slogged through early drafts, who hung with me through thick and thin and made me laugh until I cried.

Likewise to my amazing friends who pushed me to write when I wasn't sure I could, who kept on me, gently (and sometimes not-so-gently) pestering me to get a move on and eventually this book, formed out of parts and particles came to be.

I can't begin to thank Ghee, Andrea, John, Claudia, Eileen, Thoreau, Barbara, Andrew, Amanda, Davy and Sheridan enough for their time, wisdom, humor, observations, comments, critiques, and cover art for, without all of them, this book wouldn't exist.

Part 1

"It's the notion that there is no perfection–that this is a broken world and we live with broken hearts and broken lives but still that is no alibi for anything. On the contrary, you have to stand up and say hallelujah under those circumstances."

—Leonard Cohen

Confabulation

Sometimes you sleep the last hours breathing
all the night's angles, day begins on the tip of a
branch breaking. It's too early for opera. Day &
night the road is damp, anxious, drone of wheels
as they slow to stop.

We begin by talking about the birds returning
but it's not the beginning of anything anymore.
You fall into bed and morning comes, resolves,
revolves. You sleep the hours with one eye barely
open.

& yes, these are our fingerprints on the walls,
plans revolving in angles, semantics. We go
to sleep on a branch breaking. Anything is
beginning. Sometimes we work a different
resolution, slow the truth in our heads.

There are birds in your neighbor's backyard and
it's early, remember. A day in a neighborhood, a
way to talk about plans. Sometimes we fall into
bed on the tip of a branch.

Memory without a map is the beginning of
anything. And it's early remember. Truth
revolves, an opera sounds, fingerprints on the
walls look like a map, birds beginning on a
branch breaking.

Synonym for Home

1. *Abode*: Any living space is space living. We are living above the Jiffy Lube and then it's August, not much left in the refrigerator. "Look under the couch" often used in a mock-formal tone.

2. *Apartment*: A living space consisting. Coexisting. Conjuring. Conning. There's a circling, a wand of pale dolor sprinkled over the furniture. You are telling a story that involves figures I've never met. We are of one or more rooms about it, a complex unit of two.

3. *Billet*: Quarters in a private home assigned to shadows, to footsteps and military order, to "Anonymous." You have decided to grow a mustache and look so much like a deceased relative that your great aunt holds out her hand, traces her finger over your lips. "Welcome home," she says.

4. *Boardinghouse*: A house that provides some room. I sleep with one eye open. Multiple

latches and locks and an arsonist lives below, never looks me in the eye. He stares at my boots. "Those are boys shoes," he says. We stand in the kitchen, and watch our bagels burn.

5. *Bungalow*: A small one-or one-and-a-half-story house. The kind we dreamed as kids. We'd live in this bungalow with two or more rabbits, make crepes and grow lemon trees. The story ends there.

6. *Cabin*: Originally, a small, crudely constructed one-story dwelling. One made of gingerbread or graham cracker paths, a place where ovens run too hot for comfort. This one has four identical beds; four identical blue plaid comforters. Often refers to memories we've left unassigned, amorphous. Scratches on the bathroom door are courtesy of a long dead dog. A watercolor of a boat that isn't. A vacation home may be quite large or psychically complex.

7. *Caravan*: A British English synonym for trailer. In Germany after a long day fighting with her boyfriend, the mother takes

off in the Volkswagen camper, her boyfriend left to fend for himself. Exhausted, the mother parks on the outskirts of a dark town. At night there are voices quietly speaking near the van, discussing this and that. The mother whispers in her sleep.

Ways

Somewhere a satellite listens as dishes are washed, pots scrubbed. A woman hushes her children to hear the front door creak.

Bulging with conversations, uncompleted monologues, incomplete sentences. Eavesdropping from the sky. Voices condensed to a symphony of data, staccato ellipses.

Another war escalates. Caught and boosted on rabbit ear antenna. What comes down from the sky belong to anyone who can find it. There are plans to kill plans, to leave locks unlocked, abandon the hypothetical music of ghosts and walk away.

In the hallway, a pair of shoes hurries. A mother gives birth in her bathtub, biting down on a rolled up washcloth. Holding it all in so as to not disturb the sky.

What Lies Beneath

After my mother's death, Stinson Beach, 2014

There is no manual for how
to find ourselves in this world
whittled of silt and current
baffled by hurricane and storm
(offshore winds skitter over our eyelids)
No manual to explain how the heart
forms its own sandbar
to protect against erosion
in the middle of a breaking surf
or predict what exactly lies beneath the waves.

Compass

For Andrea and John

Rummaged for my husband's hand, vanished
under the surface of his breath. Inside hush &
think we'll be all right and go on dreaming.
Love's scrawl on every surface, coffee grounds,
a sticky kitchen counter, yellowed notes on
the refrigerator door, the other half of the
sandwich left for you, what we carry from
room to room.

Maybe if we rouse the story from its river,
we'll catch the refrain, muffled, telling us
to shake our doubts out in the open, trust
someone will catch us when we fall because
we fall.

Turn the compass upside down, shake the
arrow loose from its stem, let it spin. See
where it takes you & start from there.

Part 2

"An hour, once it lodges in the queer element of the human spirit, may be stretched to fifty or a hundred times its clock length."

—Virginia Woolf

Vanishing Twin

San Francisco, 1983

Belly up looking for
light otherwise
what are we here for? We think
this longing or vanishing twin
whose right lung in utero
absorbs song and coos
shooting stars before they dust
our tongues.

We disappear into quartets of our
own intent I never meant to
regret the hours' amble.
Never meant to belly up
to the gun's muzzle
listen to the trigger unlock.

Vagrant Waltz

Across a gully
between cottonwood branches
blades somersault
spines fold
slash red bark through trunks.
In this altitude
heat circles the badlands
scratches at ankles slicks the hair
suspicion runs high with
so many mouths to water. Who makes
so little a home?
There is no accurate word
for missing you nothing
summed (cooed).
In this plot air presses air
(I am never the same).

Rift

I know the guttural urge to walk the fog,
confusing it for heaven & rummage for brothers
that have stepped barefoot from memory's curb.

Which brings us back to this fog & the believers
who shake salt over their shoulders like crumbs.

An errand can take you anywhere, even into
the woods, a bridge of mothers' voices calling
through a flash flood where a path is cleared to
better hear the names.

We are all unsolved; bartering for faith with
whatever is at hand, hoping it's enough to keep
us at the table.

He hides his head but doesn't sleep. A parachute
of air and smoke gathered in the hem of his
mouth.

You know how maps recite their borders
then take on a language of ledgers, average in
the floods the oil spilled and spilt & all the
exhaustion on loan.

Who says we can only occupy one room at a
time?

Pacific, we lay our debts on the table, the
kisses and bad advice we gave so freely.

Love is quick like this. We forgive ourselves
when the rent is due & pride's just not able.

Relativity Once Removed

Reno, Nevada 2016

Clock him, my father tells my brother. He
stands at the corner of parable and history
with his cut-and-paste prayer, his lonely
hieroglyphs. He carries a backpack filled with
letters he'll never finish. When he gets to the
ocean, he turns his back on us.

On the strip, gamblers wait for daybreak and
over-easy eggs, rib-eyes the size of almanacs.
Hunger is mutable even as we try to measure
its length, the paydays blown in one fell
swoop. Days where complex maneuvers fail
to recover. Somewhere my brothers swim,
synchronized, poised in kinetic variables (that
follow the sun).

If it's true that we play dice with the
universe, then is God a reckless metaphor, a
mathematical equation composed of stars,
black holes, peripheral blood flow? Did you
clock him, my father asks. My brothers found
another way around the equation, a way to
climb into distance without actually leaving.

Here is my mother, straddling a line between faith and desertion, abandoning plans even as she unfolds a map. Restraint has failed her and it's a relief. She adapts the story, adjusts the oxygen, watches as my brothers dive into the deep end, their arms held over their heads in makeshift steeples.

Tale

The wolf snaps his jaws, swallows the girl whole—end of story. Fairy tales are revised so that darkness never falls completely. So that girls and rage are blunders in eternal dusks unfolding on the edge of the page, margins barely visible and ever after everything is eaten and the wine drunk the failure to come up with an escape route is on us. If you let your guard down the fairy tale says, if you let your hair fall from the tower.

Daughters

for Grace and Hayley

To each: their blood and blonde. We stumble
into thinning air, pockets vacant, mouths
fuming with lipstick and curses. Memory
places our city in disorder.

We wait for revelation, our spoons held high,
orchestrating the affections of this opera. At
night, I listen as you mutter through a tangle
of truths & tenderness.

We cough up what we attempt to bury,
twisted sentences, awkward excuses.

Fierce tongue, you grow taller than my fear,
outlive it by running & I worry you like a
chain of smoke, lift the word to err.

You row in the quiet dark while high on the
bank I watch through the leaves. Exhaust my
eyes waiting for a reply.

For Ann

This day is long and dogged and salt pours too easy. Rain on everything pen scrawl smudges. What makes us ferocious what makes us sigh into the night hour. Switch the lights on, make dinner, sing our daughters to sleep. This and this too will pass will stitch hours into some makeshift quilt will conceive another blessing in the world impossible weather impossible usually the heart is stupid blown away by its own hole of implausible quiver. What is usual isn't today it rains and doesn't quit pours in buckets and leaks into this frame this sepia belief.

Topology

for Grace at fifteen years old

It's a half clairvoyance, an elsewhere sun that I
brush from your hair. Tangles of shook light,
the honey of riotous bees.

You stare out the single window in your room
disguised as a stranger looking through nothing
and I trace the pitch of your silence as if I could
suspend it, draw out its vibration, its multiple
tones.

Perhaps it's your swagger perfecting the city's
streets, an unfamiliar gait that makes me hurry
into the produce market, thump the eggplants
hard against their skins.

& here's my body pitching forward, bent,
a petting zoo of animals trailing behind,
unleashed, stirring up the past, dragging their
empty bowls between their teeth, fixing me a
hungry stare.

I watch for secrets to grow tired in your pocket
and unfold them like origami birds, allow them
take off, hoping one might teach me how our
love lakes. Illegible waters. Want for anything
the oar's arc as it scrawls water and air, its
expectation. All I can't photograph.

Part 3

"I feel like I've never had a home, you know? I feel related to the country, to this country, and yet I don't know exactly where I fit in. There's always this kind of nostalgia for a place, a place where you can reckon with yourself."

—Sam Shepard

Instructions for the Eclipse

Nevada

Circle the wagons; lick your wounds under
this stone sun. When the stink bugs invade,
you'll hunt for shade, but won't find an inch.
If you decide this climate suits you, wear long
pockets. Bring a knife that can pick sand
from your teeth, skin a prickly pear. At the
turnout, there'll be a single tree with sneakers
lassoed over its branches, a note pinned to the
trunk. It'll be your last chance to turn back.
This might be a cautionary tale or include
advice on how to get clean, get home. Here,
guns repeat at the sound of a foot-drop, so be
careful how you move. Memorize the rules,
even if you rearrange their substance. There's
always something here that can't be fully seen;
forget what's been said about staring into the
sun, settle in, watch the corona flame.

Impediment

In the garden that wasn't
a meal went cold
conversation stalled
tumbleweeds blew and
caught on the tablecloth's hem.
Last night the dead wore
raincoats filled their pockets
with whatever they could
filch bottle caps, shot glasses,
rings from the river.
They gave me keys
that didn't work on my lips.

Steer Clear

This is how you excavate
probe the subject clean the pipes elbows
the woman ribs her deep
in her dank corner
working for free for nothing
is tenuous (sickle comb shears)
arrow   games there's no such thing

Rise from bed
even when gravity is
spun flax   comes down
to synonyms high voltage howl
uttered truth the way we dance our
numerous lives on a pin
remove this from the evidence
suggest a new name for (fissure family
moving)
forward steer reason to its prime
correct the data that's collected
too broad take
a picture and fail at make it talk
instead draw knots
steer clear of cats
of bluster   steer clear of static and dry
martinis of empty hallways
and obvious scents

Dinghy

Afghanistan

Weaving through summer, the war closes in
on fallen jays & my heart won't budge. On
television today a mid-season repeat of the
same fallen bird leaves us all drained. Streets
fill the hours with accidents and noise, skid
marks on the olive tree. Later there will be
birds in the trees, but not now.

We sleep our unbelief, spend secrets there,
temper the moon's stare. The hills burn
for hours on a television set that no one is
watching. Wired electric stroking moonlight's
red intention. Strip off your clothes become
my patient strand your eye here.

Mirrors refuse to hold us anymore; we keep
tap-dancing out of the frame, tripping over
claims and rejections, all in the same sentence.
Where's the dinghy? I'm taking off to see the
world.

Mosquitoes tremble over our story, thirsty
for blood. We die in each other's anecdotes,
our right hands growing cold in familiar
signatures. The birds have quit speaking, but
we can't filter out the noise.

Above us, satellites course like bloated dinghies through our dreams. Maps unravel, snapping trees at their root, reiterating their methods.

Aerial recordings are so precise you can hear jays circle the garden fountain, their soundtrack of birdsongs trailing.

Tumble Down

Reno, Nevada 2015

"I've seen birthmarks that resembled angel kisses, potatoes, eels and even hams," the woman on the roof says, pounding imaginary nails into the shingles.

Searching for an answer, the man asks the bookstore clerk, "Which one of these will give me fever? How will I know?"

We are in a new city with change in our pockets. A river runs here & our hearts don't turn to sand. You might be a beast of unseemly wishes. You might be unselective. You might be a kind-hearted kind of fool.

A tumble down light skims the desert floor. I carry binoculars around my neck, a compass hangs at my hip. There's a whole world I can't begin to pronounce.

Keep Rising

> *For my brothers, Dean and Brett, on
> the anniversaries of their deaths*

Months of bad light bruise flecks of flame
but eventually you find that overdue library
book and then without meaning to, she finds
you on the street, crouched, your gun cocked,
aiming high into the eucalyptus. She doesn't
know you'd rather surrender and not ready
for another winter this one's gone on in black
hems & you'll understand when her roots
grow out coarse, unruly. There's nothing but
wait it out. Satellites hover above with their
hiss and rumble. She figures in numbers that
refuse to add up. They tremble in the back of
her head & water keeps rising.

Flood Zone

For Arthur Moss

There's this story of my father. He sits on his family's porch swing, shucking corn, Detroit isn't twitchy yet. Later, his bare feet push over the floorboards while he picks over another ear, scatters salt from end to end and bites down into the raw sweet flesh. This is his version of heaven, not yet panged by insurrection. More corn than he can ever.

Rough Draft for April

For Eric on our wedding anniversary

We are west & more than blood. Coyote brush, ice plant, greasewood. Only reason we came to roost is love—sometimes inside promises thin as twigs. Make a nest with whatever's left. Take pains to leave a tune. It's almost April and there's mint growing wild somewhere.

Intermezzo & Single Tanka

For my mother, Ann Moss

I couldn't save you
from this coup of crazy
its syllables branching out across this land
rambling, and that's not the worst of it
I couldn't save myself.
What is it you're trying to say &
I don't know anymore.

At the edge of this neglected rose
garden of bifurcated thorn and browning branch
past soil the color of wood ash, a cottonwood tree,
full of June sheds across public
boundaries, splashes a reverse Rorschach
of white over the Truckee River.

Your bed levitates
at night, you believe, a zeppelin
rising above this nursing
home, leaving it all behind.

Pull of memory's halftones,
& large-scale absences mean that
only a plumb line can begin to measure
amnesia's depth, the steep slope
of evaporation as one western
season ends and vapor beads

rise above the earth's core
out of the electric chatter's frame.

A photograph scaled to fit a family
momentarily removes displacement.
Tilt & relief.

Everything happens
outside this pair of photos
fugues overlap
please don't step too far to the left
the frame cannot hold you.

I try to recall a line map
of birthdays, of roads
reeled, your gray eyes, language
soughed in ungentle sloping,
crowding numbers on a clock,
surprising time.

(or were they blue?)
A drawing composed of
subdivided lines, of meter.

Particular boundaries are singular.
Particular memory is entered.
Tides move particularly
inside a full moon, neurons firing
reconstructing a map of
syntax and confabulation.

Red-tailed hawks glide
the currents of your mind-sky,
you shoo them away
with a sweep of your hand.
I watch the river
recede in inches, listen as stones
clatter across this deafening shore.

Sagebrush, rabbitbrush, greasewood and willow;
dolls, card games, cadenza—a fervent gleaning of
names, this certain sweeping away.

Under is another story
with vowels bright, spit-shined,
particular as sudden singular
as we brim & yield from
one room to the next.

Hem

> *Crossville, Tennessee from a photo of my grandmother, Annabelle, and her sisters*

Sisters anchor their hems with the flat of their
palms, each shoulder and hip thrust angled
to sever the photographer's intent. Now,
memorized as forever disinclined, jammed
into focus. An emblem of their frequent
commotion: what's been whispered across
hallways & jarred up for stretches. Next year
when the wind seizes, it'll knock the tripod
flat into the heirloom roses, split the camera
open, a length of film will snake the cool
green grass. Sisters' hair will drift out from
bobby pins, gold tipped, fervent.

Open Space

For Art Moss

Heaven aims to crowd out the blue sky of
my mouth. We are all a little harmed. Night
lowers, snakes past fences past strangers
waiting on a hallelujah.

On the walls of loss & lack, my font breaks
down to a broken song. I carve our names to
claim them, each letter imagined.

Scribbled with ghosts, my heart draws outside
the lines, polishes a joke until the punch
line shines. When I'm wading these waters,
I pretend to swim while you walk the river's
edge where glass-bottomed boats skin the
water like smoke.

I came here to flirt, spill your secrets, make
confetti of your death, your life—all the burn
& tango.

Keep It Together

Los Gatos, 1975

Every three miles for nearly seventy they pour
water into the radiator, feed the leak.

Her muddy hem & knife tucked into his belt
spells out why best-laid plans go awry.

A hornet's nest gets hit & the air grows
silvery.

Sometimes a body can't tell fiction from fact.

Radiator's got a crack he says. No shit
Sherlock.

Whether it is lake our memories lack or
forgiveness nobody gets to go back.

There's not enough.

Empty Your Pockets

Advice for Hayley as she travels

Our mouths plink plank blackstrap, chip & peel.
Goodbyes are seldom clean.

Wipe the mud from the mirror so we can see
where we've been.

From here no one can see
the last footfall before hibernation
hear the bony water collect under rocks.

Once I would have waited
for letters, phone calls even the
green laugh of dismissal. Once
I would wait white-lipped.

The plan is to climb this wall
& rappel out wide
leave these oil-stained feathers
where the river empties.
Not wear this fray so public.

All cartography is smudged
graphite borders, spilt waters
lambs saddled for a long trip.

In this puckered light
roads pitch forward
in every direction. Pick one &

Empty your pockets at night
keep change in a jar near your bed
take your shoes off at thresholds
borrow what you need.
If a drone dangles too close
to your window find a broom,
shoo it away.

Underscore

Some have a way of getting under your skin &
hold your memory out like a bowl.

You can't come uninvited.

Just around the corner, my clarity smudged
under so much rain (it sucks to say goodbye)
you close your door.

What doesn't break will make you thread
ampersands in the air.

With all that's left between tomorrow should
bring a package.

A porkpie hat, a note tucked into its brim.
A quarter bag of chocolate chips.
A light bulb wrapped in one of your socks.

Little Bombs

The end isn't a surprise you dole out
for strangers, the small coins in your pocket.
The world's little bombs have gone off & now
you're gone.

Look at this neighborhood of open windows;
how long will it take to settle these hands?

Crack the code of these dreamless years. Whir
of the camera continues in the machinery's
absence. Scratched where penlight gathers &
unfolds—a fluid origami of secrets, exhausted.

Consider our own invention without
measure, directionless. I've only come to say
there's a kiss on the mirror for you to find
before we fall again.

There/Enough

Where you lay your nose
to the ground, a thundering,
horse hooves in your nostrils,
gravel spit
lost no more.
A bird-call from outside
horizon's thin demarcation

\#

A city drowns or is bullied
shot to pieces its mouth cracked open
in perpetual surprise

\#

Boiling under where blood
invites gusts to enter
history confused by memory or lost
in evidence

\#

As unlikely hosts
we can't be pilgrims
at this dinner
can't stick an apple in the pig's
mouth and call it a day
these prayers are, if not broken, less able
& these descendants? Where do they sit?
What does it mean to pray without ceasing?

#

I gave up my pipe
early on couldn't keep the tobacco lit
its purpose was lost in ritual
in evening's flint & promise
of conversations that came in drafts

#

Posturing in the rain still
as a kite with two winds
gathered at my throat
What keeps us standing
holding up a spoon
and handful of grubby herbs?
What keeps us offering
praise as the river appears
to rise over maxim and eye?

\#

You write the governor a note
asking for clemency
you do not beg & won't
lie in the dead grass and cry
an open letter to the world
it would be unfortunate
a dialysis where pings pang and move
on at first blush
the sugar highs and gentle
quacking of machines left
to their own corners and devices
A symphony revealed in grace

\#

Take your valley back
it wasn't mine anymore anyway
shoot salt at shadows,
pick from high branches
whatever fruit is there
sourgrass road
skins of bicycle tires strung
over eucalyptus
that smell a little like home

\#

River road and ridden
rounded rocks winter finally
and done with such summer's
skulk in the undergrowth of bridge sighs
where earnest secrets tied to beds
go bone-dry

\#

A fluorescent sign hiccups
a slightly queasy red
over the avenue   we pass
slowly now there's a window
filling with sand then another
Sleep it off we can try again tomorrow.

Heresy

On my birthday

Mirror glimpses
converges at your hips &
thighs (all this slipping into place
to place ourselves).
At night the needle digs
repeats this deep shipwreck
song (you are so lovely you are you are).

Year of the Bumblebee

year of salvia & un-celestial
hummingbird
Year of the chronic cough &
a string of rejections
kiss & telling in the dark
It is the year of decomposition
of ground games
battles over personal
topography   It is the year of one step back
& twist to the hips
A banner year for nefarious weeds
the rigged righteous   for water

Four-Minute Warning

I hear on the radio that in three minutes the
world as we know it will be gone, but doesn't
that happen every day—to be someone and
say goodbye to the peacetime speaking clock?
An everyday frequency, an advertisement
or hand powered sirens whistle the safest
place is indoors there is nothing to be gained
by running away. I hear on the radio water
bottles rolling. There is a blue sound, a needle
dropping from a child's hand, rush of leaves,
remember crossed out from the original copy.

*The four-minute warning was a public alert system
conceived by the British Government
during the Cold War.*

Wyrd

for Ann Moss

Told you would someday have a Viking
funeral, you went to sleep dreaming of
longships & fire but all I could come up with
on that windy day under the Golden Gate
was a frail leaf, a milk jar of your gray ash.

Even the matches were flimsy, not at all what
you dreamed, a rite, a ceremony (the dead to
rise anew) arrows of slung flame, the slam &
slap of air against smoke striking into blaze.

Maybe I should have tried to tuck in some
earthly good, a harpsichord key, your cheetah
glasses to see the way.

Dyfed's ground has been turned over, bladed,
staked out with small bright orange flags
where the city plans on shortly rolling sod
over your son's ashes, over the wild lilies. A
tree stump pulled like a tooth lies on its side,
roots twisted, revenant, stretching upward.

Read me, place a cushion under my head
while I lie drunk (one letter at a time).

There must be places to kneel to give all,
unzip the stringed heart and strum it naked,
thrummed, raise our memory & turn the
business at hand give permission to the
deceased to find their way

There will be a ship on a leaf and your ashes
will glide, swallow the ocean.

Recitation

For Dean and Brett

Home was a sharp noise in training films
don't drop the baby and remember to
close the back door, an insidious map
of one potato two potato if I told you all the
gerrymandering that went on to
guarantee your survival all the terrain
we had to cover

If I convert the film to video and replace
the evenings with grainy images
of more honest battles
instead of this slow-mo migration of
birds, insects, humans moving steadily
somewhere out of this reference
instead of this moment
which is not chosen is not
common to our behavior

The mantra of this household
is left to interpretation
emergency numbers scrawled
on the backs of envelopes receipts
for meals eaten stuffed into
ceramic bowls, a whole bunch
of ghosts chattering then drawing
their initials in wet cement

The orchard's trashed
there was no last fall
no tree in the forest sound
just my mouth went dry
and throat tightened when it was gone

maybe we never grow
an appetite for disappearances
maybe it's why we've never trusted magic

It's Easter when the Pontiac goes
up in flames blue convertible California
dreamin'
not one person asks me to dance
on the burning hood heat runs
from my fingertips
to my heart

This is my city of ghosts knocking
back their adventures
one bowlegged tavern at a time
creating tantrums
for the way I've backlit them
in beach days dipped their feet in seaweed
We call home as much as anyone, I suppose

I'd like to say stick around
but what remains is muffled amorphous
To hell with it tell it under a different light
keep the tape going check the batteries

twice before we talk again
Man, we slayed those afternoon waves
under salt stung amendments
under star broken beauty
rebellious as a crowd without
an appetite for blood but for love
its simple circumference

I could barely carry
myself, brother and was thinking
about stairs and stars
how I could tell the story
of how we met again

Church

Jimmy the lock
of the shack's back door.
All it takes is a bobby
pin and spit. Enter
this threshold. Beloved,
we've been left
behind in salvation
cuts our words bright surface
when we kiss.

Part 4

"We went our separate ways, but within walking distance of one another."

—Patti Smith, *Just Kids*

How to Canter Under Anesthesia

Renown Hospital, ICU—Reno, Nevada

This is how we roll.
Lightning, a starfish in our eye or gun
fired synapsis before going
under another wave.

We wail thread
our forearms with initials
veins slit wounded blue.

Smooth the grass down smooth
our heartbeats against the blade.
When our palms unfold
we can read the future.

Excuse me if there's something
I need. Your blood runs hot, you say
rattles through these stories.

This is not the first time
I've lost to faith or faith
has lost to me.

The river freezes
my arteries drag me
under painless anaesthetised

and I emerge rock torn bone
scraped waiting to be
wrung out left to dry on the shore.

This is how we roll.
I thought your shadow was
a ghost or maybe moving
out of any frame of reference.

Dig deep, scrape like snakes
amid memory's seams.
I've stopped looking
for omens except occasionally
when the moon evacuates the sky
and stars tip at the Sierra's edge.

Or when I touch you
& all the poisons that vein
my breasts momentarily wane.

There is just this, my body
of stitched horses cantering
proceeding without
a compass, only stars.

Radiotherapy

> *Institute for Cancer—Reno, Nevada*

Even a hundred calendars of sky don't prepare
us wounds are unpredicted pre-medicated
like dreaming of having one's fortune told
and then waking with ink under your nails

Whatever it takes to make this thirst go
teeth chipped from opening bottles with
back molars & as far as the horses go
they're tattooed on my hips canter
across my breasts a scorched I

Today we don't bother unpeeling
the oranges today we grin through it all

When we beg to differ voices rise
forgotten crescendo an orchestra of splintered
necks and suffering pedals notes belied
by what is gone negated sunk.

How we fail

From our chairs to watch the moon
rise into the high desert air

And horses canter alongside
the train track
miles of junk metal rust
under a long sun

In the back of the car
"Over the Rainbow" plays
shadows ping the window at 100 mph

27th Letter

For Ann, braving Lewy body dementia

Memory planed of its splinters, so long
wading in & out of love. Lure the heart out
from its shape and we run aground, wrecked
in such simple otherwise.

Anchored in undeclared depths, she sleeps
inside an earlier chance. Some nights we
dance on shrapnel, some nights we dodge
regret.

Behind thin curtains, science is evoked
through machines that blink & chorus: a
mass of spells coerced from arm's length.

We've been here long enough to understand
the scrub jay's zeep-scolds, their cacophony.

A wild barren where the soul is freshly hewn.

I make up dark stories of my Iowa birth; retell
the black ice of childhood, a skidding from
one season to the next.

History operates in waters of heresy, a snowy
alphabet where vagrancy is expected.

She shudders at the heat, flanked by nurses
& mumblings, in waters so irrefutable we can
barely remember the distances towed, the
green loss of language. One minute to the
next is approximately the same and depends
so much upon the view.

Perch

Nothing is awake yet not water or regret
not the head waiter at the now defunct hotel
circling jobs in broken sleep or the dishwasher
his cracked fingers throbbing
not the sweeper of failed
parades damp confetti under her nails
orbiting the worn lobby of her dreams
waiting for her number to be called.

Anywhere At All

A synonym for home is
a stern description an unlikely
bit of luck struck
between dusks.

A bedroom with drawers
where I can think of you
when I want, never finishing.

Knowing where you
come from isn't anywhere at all.

An Undoing

Apricot orchard in Cupertino, California—1967

1.

In the sequence
that was cut from the story
you don't know the wretched
shadow that hung from the branch
husked light dimming
on these words living side
by side.

Maybe the patent leather shoe was found
covered in mud near a tree
trunk painted pink or maybe
our frame of reference changed
the shoe holding little importance
to a story unraveling
at the edge of an orchard
saccharine rot of
apricots, then another shoe
spoiling among the flies.

2.

After all that, the orchard's gone
there was no last fall
no tree in the forest crash
just my mouth went dry

and throat tightened to see sunlight
scrambling to find a branch but only
finding a row of identical framed houses.

Then flashes of grace when least expected
red-tailed hawk circling above
on a string of wind
a remembered name
works its way to the surface
and that day there's a letter
saying everything's fine.

I was thinking
about starting your story
from the beginning
and when we meet again
I won't disappoint you
and you'll uncross your legs
add a few details and we can
carve our names into the bench
sit, say nothing.

She Took Off Her Girdle

When you are married, she said, words
are walnut shells, living tissue whose cells
have soft walls and the capacity for growth.
The husk is complicated. Tasting faintly of
caramel and anise. A walnut tree needs deep
fertile soil to grow.

But no one listens, there is an assembly of old
ideas in the wide wood, some kind of smack
talk, and she moves further into winter,
stroking its surface for a place she can breathe,
unencumbered. When spring eventually
appears, and the sun hauls itself into the sky,
a butterfly trails from her threaded waist,
colors brimming. Miracles are scrupulous,
often fragile things, synonymous with truths
that can topple kingdoms. Find the good and
praise it.

A red thread falls on a leaf and she shivers,
not because she's cold, on the contrary, she
knows how fever girds her blood, fringes her
hip bones. She cracks open a walnut, spreads
a blanket across its inner shell, pulls the satin
trim over her head, belts her waist with the
thread. Getting ready for the ride.

The dead parachute into her dreams,
unflappable, adding to this story from a short
distance, or sometimes rest in her dreams
like migratory swallows, their eyes shut,
wings swooned, their hearts looping into
hers, stitching one generation to another.
When you are married, she said, occasionally
walnuts drop into empty courtyards, barely
making a clunk and sometimes they are
gathered, their meat dipped in honey.

About the Author

Michelle Murphy is a writer who lives in Reno, Nevada. She's lived in a van, on the edge of a creek, in a shotgun flat in North Beach, and now lives at the top of a highrise above the Truckee River that she shares with her husband, daughter and mean-ish cat. She believes a writer should put out at least one book every 25 years and so is right on schedule with her second book, *Synonym for Home*. Her first book *Jackknife & Light* (Avec Books) was shortlisted for the National Poetry Series. More information can be found at https://murphypoetry.wordpress.com/

Wet Cement Press Titles

Series 1

My Dog, Me (novel), Anthony Schlagel
ISBN 978-1-7324369-3-0 (2019)

Saraswati's Lament (poetry), Barbara Roether
ISBN 978-1-7324369-0-9 (2019)

Synonym for Home (poetry), Michelle Murphy
ISBN 978-1-7324369-2-3 (2019)

Wilson Wiley Variations (poetry), Thoreau Lovell
ISBN 978-1-7324369-1-6 (2019)

www.ingramcontent.com/pod-product-compliance
Lightning Source LLC
Chambersburg PA
CBHW030236100526
44584CB00015BB/1525